GUITAR ATLAS SERIES

Guitar Styles from Around the Globe

Jamaica

Your passport to a new world of music

Approved Curriculum

RALEIGH GREEN

Alfred, the leader in educational music publishing,

and the National Guitar Workshop,

one of America's finest guitar schools, have joined

forces to bring you the best, most progressive

educational tools possible. We hope you will enjoy

this book and encourage you to look for

other fine products from Alfred and the

National Guitar Workshop.

Alfred

Alfred Music Publishing Co., Inc.
16320 Roscoe Blvd., Suite 100
P.O. Box 10003
Van Nuys, CA 91410-0003
alfred.com

ISBN-10: 0-7390-6281-6 (Book & CD)
ISBN-13: 978-0-7390-6281-4 (Book & CD)

*This book was acquired, edited, and produced
by Workshop Arts, Inc., the publishing arm of
the National Guitar Workshop.
Nathaniel Gunod, acquisitions, managing editor
Burgess Speed, acquisitions, senior editor
Timothy Phelps, interior design
Barbara Smolover, interior illustrations
Ante Gelo, music typesetter
CD recorded and mastered by Collin Tilton at Bar None Studio, Northford, CT
Raleigh Green (guitar), Matthew Liston (bass), Pete Sweeney (drums)*

*Cover photographs:
Ocho Rios, Jamaica © Winston Davidian / istockphoto
Guitar courtesy of Gibson USA*

Contents

Track
1

A compact disc is included with this book. Using it with the book can make learning easier and more enjoyable. The symbol shown at the left appears next to every example that is on the CD. Use the CD to help ensure that you're capturing the feel of the examples and interpreting the rhythms correctly. The track number below the symbol corresponds directly to the example you want to hear. Track 1 will help you tune to this CD. Enjoy!

About the Author

Raleigh Green, based in the Boston area, is known for his versatility as a guitarist and his expertise as a music educator. Proficient in many styles of music, Raleigh is the author of *The Versatile Guitarist* (Alfred/National Guitar Workshop #28243). He teaches guitar at Phillips Academy in Andover, Massachusetts and is a long-time instructor for the National Guitar Workshop and DayJams. Raleigh teaches online guitar lessons at WorkshopLive.com and is endorsed by D'Addario strings. After receiving a B.F.A. from the University of Missouri with a concentration in art and computer-aided multimedia, Raleigh attended the Berklee College of Music where he graduated *summa cum laude* and was awarded both the Quincy Jones Award and the Professional Music Achievement Award. Raleigh lives in Medford, Massachusetts with his wife, Laura, their son Cole, and an Australian cattle dog named Max.

PHOTO BY BILL SAMPLE COURTESY OF WORKSHOPLIVE.COM

ACKNOWLEDGEMENTS

Very special thanks to Laura and Cole, Ken and Linda Green, the Breretons, and all of my friends, students, and colleagues at Phillips Andover Academy; David, Barbara, and Jesse Smolover; Burgess Speed, and everyone else in the Workshop family. Also thanks to Kevin "K-Don" Michaels, Wayne Marshall, and Carl Johnson for research assistance; D'Addario & Co.; and Pete Sweeney and Matthew Liston for playing great music on the CD.

This book is dedicated to Cole Leven Brereton-Green.

NOTATION GUIDE

H = Hammer-on.

P = Pull-off.

SL = Ascending slide.

SL = Descending slide.

P.M. = Palm Mute.

⌢ = *Fermata.* Pause, or hold note longer than its indicated duration.

> = *Accent.* Emphasize the note or chord.

♩ = *Staccato.* Make note shorter than its indicated duration.

✕ = *Chuck.* Muted, percussive, unpitched note.

p, i, m, a = The right-hand fingers starting with the thumb.

1, 2, 3, 4, 0 = The left-hand fingers starting with the index finger; 0 = open string. The left-hand fingers are indicated under the TAB.

rit. = Abbreviation for ritardando. Become gradually slower.

Swing 8ths = Eighth notes written like straight eighth notes, but played with a long-short rhythm that produces the shuffle feel. When *Swing 8ths* appears at the beginning of a piece, eighth notes are played like triplets with the first two eighth notes tied (♫ = ♩♪).

♩ = 185 = Tempo marking. In this case, there are 185 quarter notes, or beats, per minute. (If you have a metronome, set it to 185).

4x = Play four times.

D.S. al Fine = *Dal Segno al Fine.* Go back to the symbol 𝄋 and play to the Fine, which is the end of the piece.

‖: :‖ = *Repeat signs.* Repeat music between the two symbols. When only the end repeat sign is present, repeat music from the beginning.

Introduction

Guitar Atlas: Jamaica is an introduction to the rich musical tradition of
Jamaica. From a guitarist's perspective, there is much to love in Jamaican
music, especially the guitar-centric styles of mento, ska, rocksteady, and
reggae. In this book, the most important Jamaican musicians, guitarists, styles,
and techniques are demonstrated through numerous musical examples. Most of these
examples are meant to be played with a pick, although there is some fingerpicking as
well. You will get the most from this book if you have experience reading standard
music notation and/or TAB, as well as some experience with common open chords,
barre chords, and basic guitar technique. The Notation Guide on page 3 should help
you with any unfamiliar notation. Welcome to *Guitar Atlas: Jamaica,* and let's begin
our journey!

JAMAICAN HISTORY

The island of Jamaica is located in the Caribbean Sea. It is situated 90 miles south of
Cuba and is a part of the Greater Antilles, a group of islands that also includes Puerto
Rico and Hispaniola. With a tumultuous history of slavery, war, poverty, and natural
disasters, Jamaica is a true melting pot of mixed ethnicities. Jamaica is smaller than the
state of Connecticut, however, the global impact that this Caribbean island has had on
the rest of the world is enormous.

When Christopher Columbus first arrived to Jamaica in 1494, the native Arawak people
(also known as Taino Indians) had already been there since 650 A.D. Sadly, soon after
Spain's occupation of the country began in 1509, the indigenous population was wiped
out by slavery, disease, and war. By 1655, Britain seized Jamaica and soon, through
intense colonization and a booming slave trade, Jamaica became the largest producer
of sugar in the world. After many uprisings, slavery was abolished in 1838. In 1872,
Kingston became the capitol, and in 1962, Jamaica became an independent nation.

JAMAICAN MUSIC OVERVIEW

In the early 19th century, when the percussive musical traditions brought over by West
African slaves mixed with the music of the European *quadrille* (a precursor to the square
dance), the Jamaican folk music style called *mento* was born. Mento was Jamaica's most
popular music throughout the 1930s and 1940s; however, during this period, American
jazz also became immensely popular in Jamaica. By the 1950s, mento was still alive,
but American R&B had largely taken hold of the Jamaican popular music scene. In
the 1960s, all of these various influences came together to create a unique Jamaican
musical style called *ska.*

The quick tempo of ska was a reflection of the upbeat mood in Jamaica after gaining
independence in 1962. Jamaicans soon observed, however, that serious social problems
remained, and in 1966, the music changed with the mood. A new style called *rocksteady*
emerged, replacing the upbeat pace of ska with a much slower feel. A short-lived
movement, rocksteady was only around for two years when Jamaica's most famous
musical style, *reggae,* was born. From the late 1960s to the mid-1980s, reggae became
a worldwide sensation. During this time period, the *Rastafari* (those belonging to
the religious and cultural *Rastafari movement* covered on page 33) garnered a strong
association with reggae due to the international fame of Bob Marley and others. English
bands like The Clash and The Police started to incorporate reggae sounds into their own
music. By the latter half of the 20th century, a wide array of reggae subgenres developed,
including *dancehall, toasting, dub, raggamuffin, reggaeton, 2-tone,* and *lovers rock,* just to
name a few. Despite being a small island, Jamaica and its varied musical traditions have
greatly inspired and influenced musicians and music lovers throughout the world.

Chapter 1 MENTO

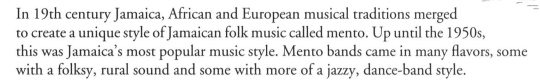
JAMAICA

HISTORY OF MENTO

In 19th century Jamaica, African and European musical traditions merged to create a unique style of Jamaican folk music called mento. Up until the 1950s, this was Jamaica's most popular music style. Mento bands came in many flavors, some with a folksy, rural sound and some with more of a jazzy, dance-band style.

The rural mento musicians played Jamaican country music, using acoustic instruments such as the banjo on lead and rhythm, acoustic guitar on rhythm, homemade bamboo saxophone (see illustration below), hand percussion, and a rumba box (see below) playing the bass notes. The more polished urban mento style was influenced by 1920s Caribbean jazz bands; instead of homemade instruments, professional saxophones and upright basses were favored, along with piano and electric guitar.

In 1951, thanks to recording pioneer Stanley Motta, the Jamaican music industry was born with the creation of the first mento record, a medley of mento songs by Bertie Lyons (also known as Lord Fly). During this period, many recordings of rural and urban mento music were produced. However, *calypso* (an Afro-Caribbean musical style from Trinidad) was the Caribbean's main musical export, so even though mento and calypso are distinct styles, the early mento recordings were sometimes called "calypsos" in order to appeal to the international music market. As the Jamaican recording industry developed, mento artists gained new exposure, riding on the wave of singer Harry Belafonte's calypso craze. The 1950s were often considered mento's "golden age," partially because of this association with calypso music, but also because of the increase in recording during that decade. This chapter takes a look at the styles of a few of the main contributors to these classic mento recordings.

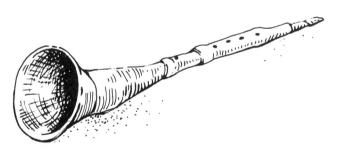

Homemade bamboo saxophone.

Rumba box.

MENTO STRUMMING

This first example is written in the style of a classic mento tune called "Naughty Little Flea." The original song was composed and recorded in the late 1950s by the internationally renowned singer, composer, dancer, and guitarist Lord Flea. Born Norman Thomas in Kingston, Jamaica in 1932, Lord Flea was sometimes called the "Calypso King of Jamaica." The arrangement below demonstrates a common mento rhythm guitar part, featuring downstrums (⊓), alternate strums (⊓ V), and common open chords. "Naughty Little Flea" went on to be covered by numerous artists, most notably Miriam Makeba and Calypso legend Harry Belafonte. (Notice on the CD the guitar is panned to the left. By turning your balance control to the right, you can eliminate the guitar part and play along with the backing band. On the CD, all examples with just one guitar are mixed this way.)

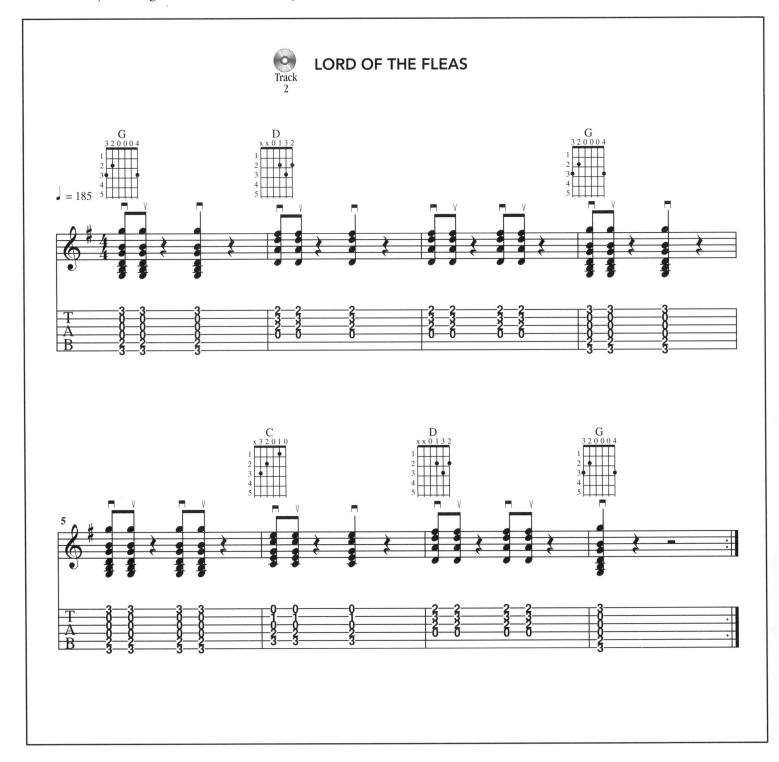

LORD OF THE FLEAS

The next example from the golden age of mento is in the style of "Glamour Gal" by Harold Richardson and The Ticklers. "Glamour Gal" was one of the first mento records ever recorded, featuring only guitar, hand percussion, and vocals. Notice in the strumming pattern the emphasis placed on beats 2 and 4; this rhythmic pulse laid the foundation for ska, rocksteady, and reggae.

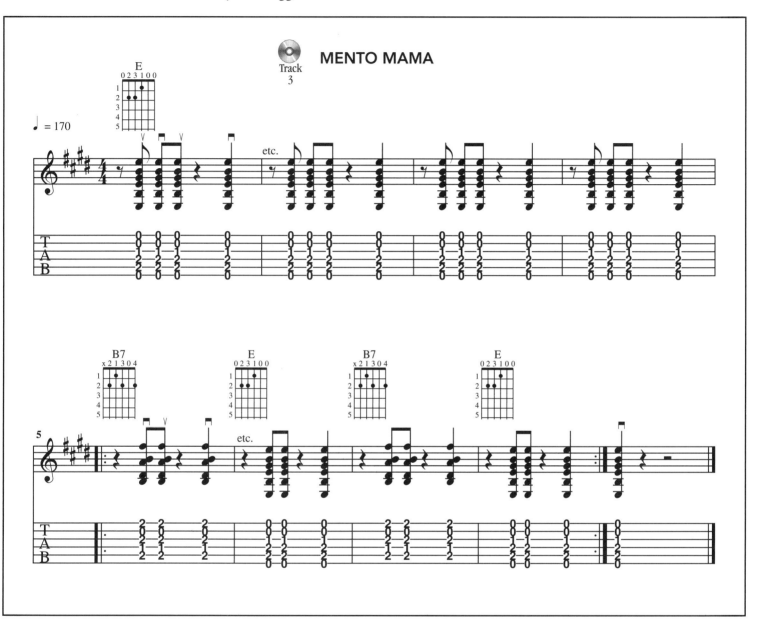

MENTO LEAD MELODIES

The Jolly Boys are one of the most notable and enduring mento bands. Although their personnel has changed numerous times throughout the years, they have been going strong from the 1940s to today. "Facing Forward" (next page) is an early mento tune in the style of "Back to Back" by The Jolly Boys. In mento, the banjo often has the role of a lead instrument due to its volume and sharp timbre (tone), which allows it to easily cut through the band. In "Facing Forward," the interplay between the acoustic rhythm guitar and the banjo (arranged as a guitar part) is illustrated. The lead melody (Guitar 1) consists of *arpeggios* (an arpeggio is the notes of a chord played separately) that alternate between eighth notes and quarter-note triplets. The rhythm guitar strumming pattern (Guitar 2) features alternate strums exclusively. (On the CD, Guitar 1 is panned to the left and Guitar 2 is panned to the right. Turn your balance control all the way left or right to isolate either part and play along with the recording. All examples with two guitars are mixed this way.)

FACING FORWARD

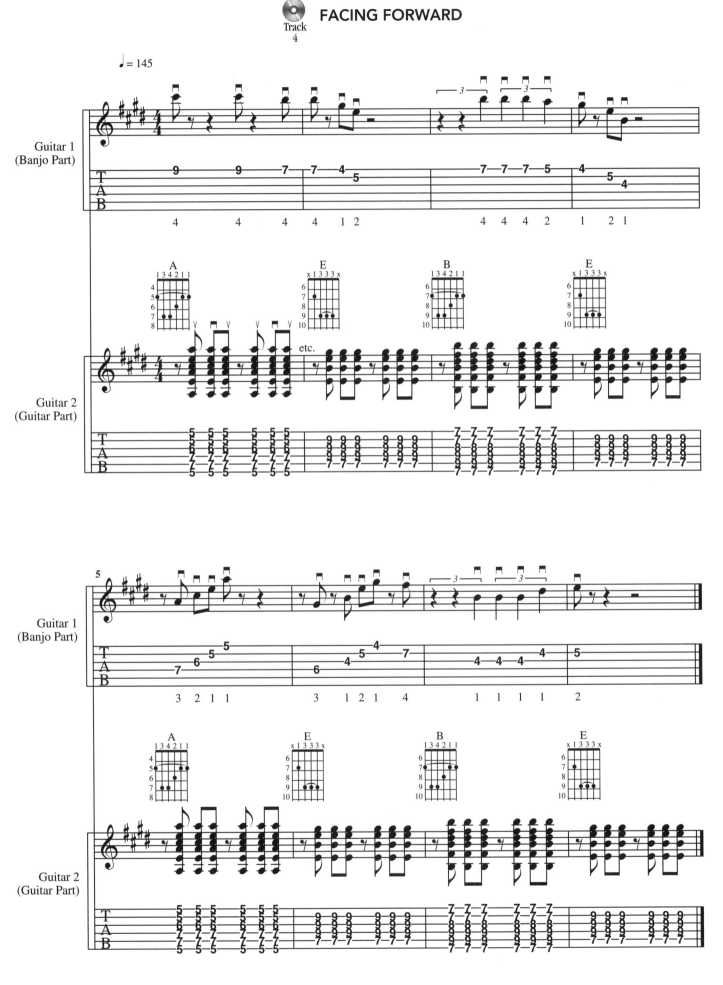

The next two examples are in the style of Count Lasher (born Terence Parkins). Count Lasher was one of the most popular and talented golden age mento stars, rivaled only by Lord Flea. He was also one of the most prolific artists, making at least 50 recordings throughout the 1950s, '60s, and '70s. The tune below is written in the style of "Samfi Man" (a "samfi man" is a con artist). Like the previous example, the banjo part (Guitar 1) plays an arpeggio-based melody, while the acoustic guitar (Guitar 2) plays a common mento strumming pattern. Remember, like all of the two- and three-part examples in this book, you can adjust your balance control and play along with either part on your CD.

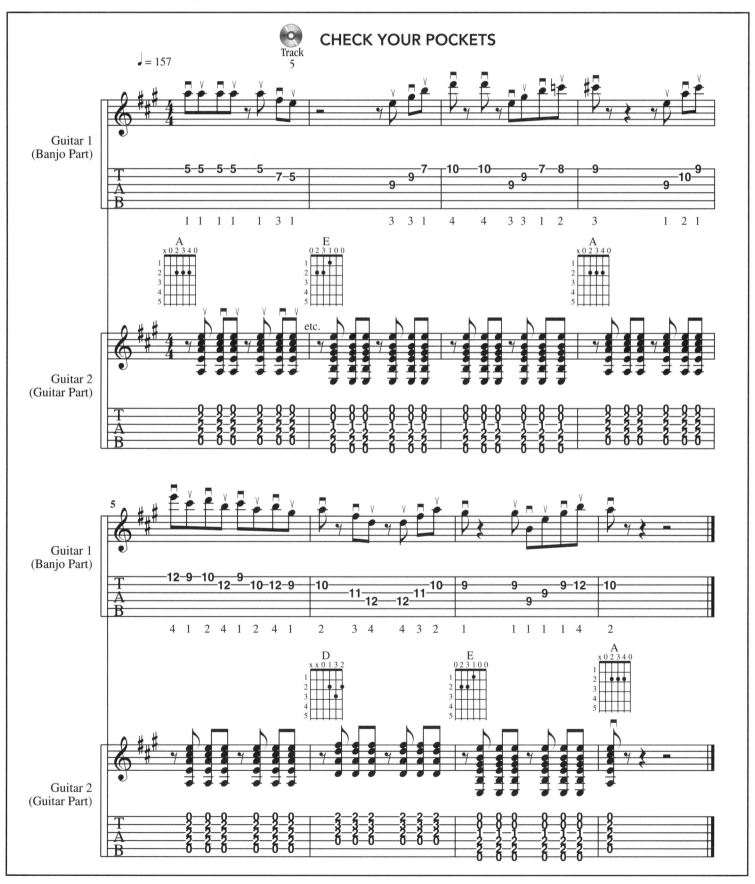

CHECK YOUR POCKETS

Following is an example based on Count Lasher's rural mento classic "Mango Time." It features a longer song form with a fingerstyle acoustic guitar intro (Guitar 2). After playing the intro, Guitar 2 switches to a mento strumming pattern that, decades later, would become an essential reggae strumming pattern (see pages 36 and 39). Since the intro is played fingerstyle, it will be necessary to strum the following rhythm patterns with either your thumb or fingers, rather than with a pick.

The lead melody (Guitar 1) is a guitar arrangement in the style of what was played on a homemade bamboo saxophone on the original recording. Notice the last phrase of this lead line, which consists entirely of quarter-note triplets. When played along with the strumming pattern based on eighth notes, this quarter-note triplet rhythm creates a compelling polyrhythmic effect that is common in mento music. (A *polyrhythm* consists of two or more independent rhythms played simultaneously.)

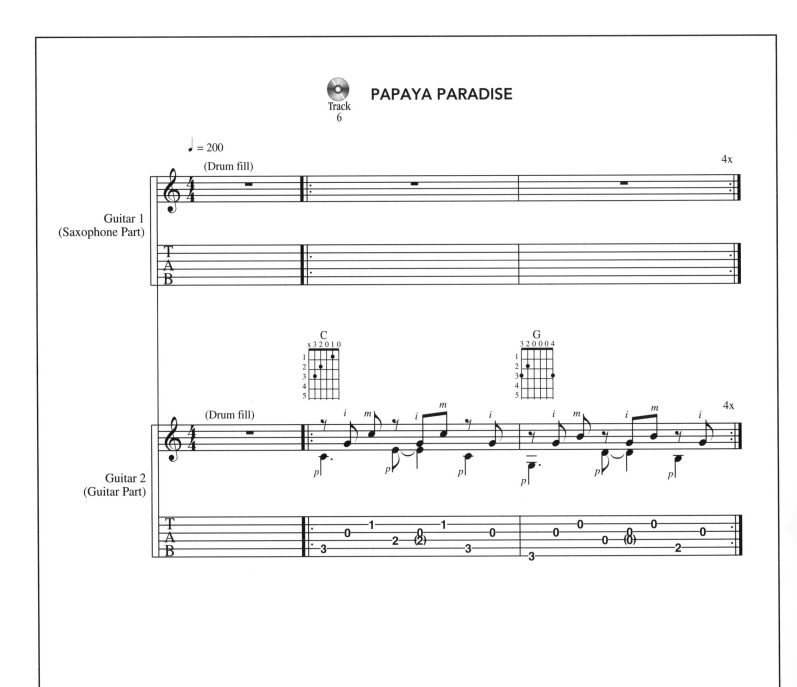

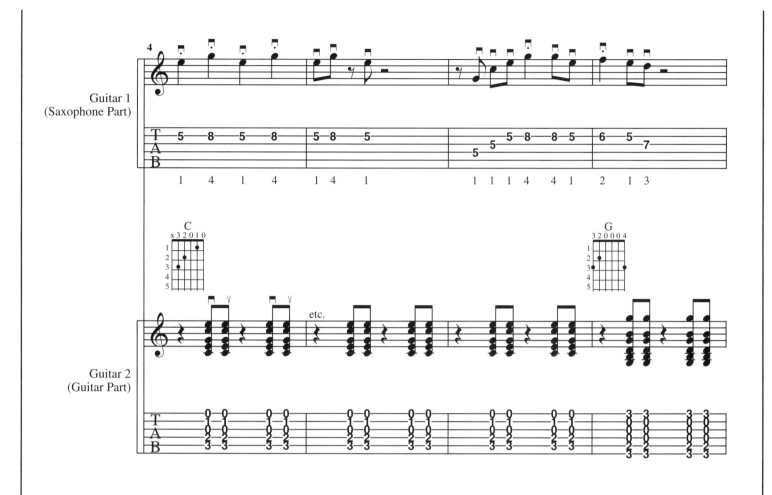

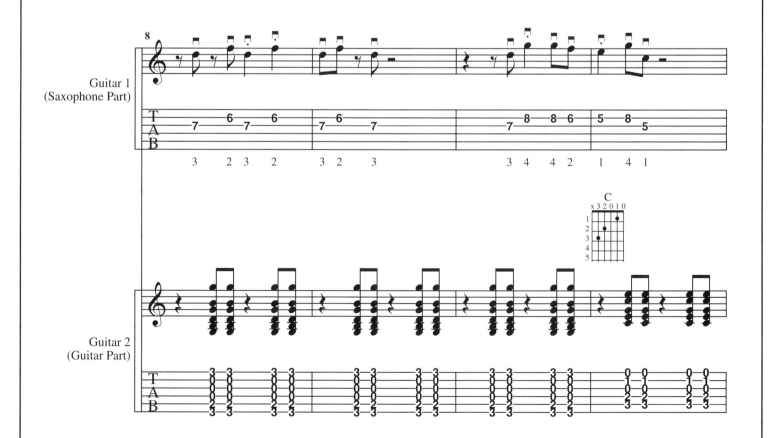

11

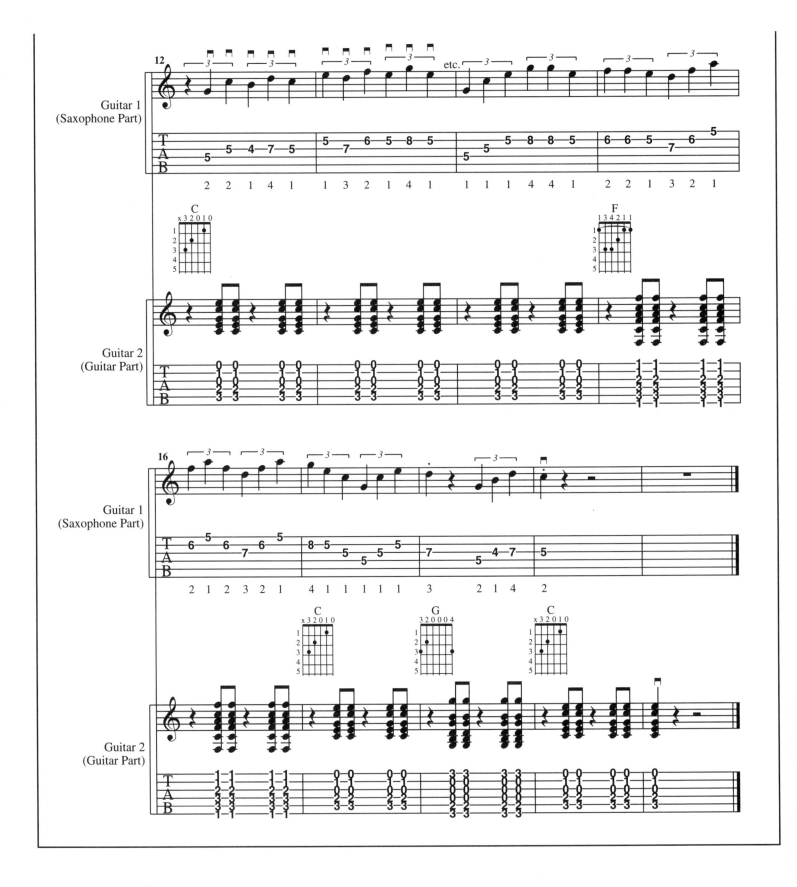

MENTO-CALYPSO

This final mento example (on the next page) is written in the style of "A Dash of the Sunshine" by Lord Tanamo. Lord Tanamo (Joseph Gordon), born in 1934 in Kingston, Jamaica, started out as a mento singer and rumba box player before going on to become one of the first lead singers of the legendary ska band The Skatalites. This is a unique tune because it contains mento, calypso, and jazz influences even though it was recorded in 1978, long after the golden age of mento had passed. It is a challenging piece to play due to the sophisticated strumming pattern and a dense, quickly moving chord progression. This song uses three-note chord voicings often found in ska and reggae styles.

COLOR ME CALYPSO

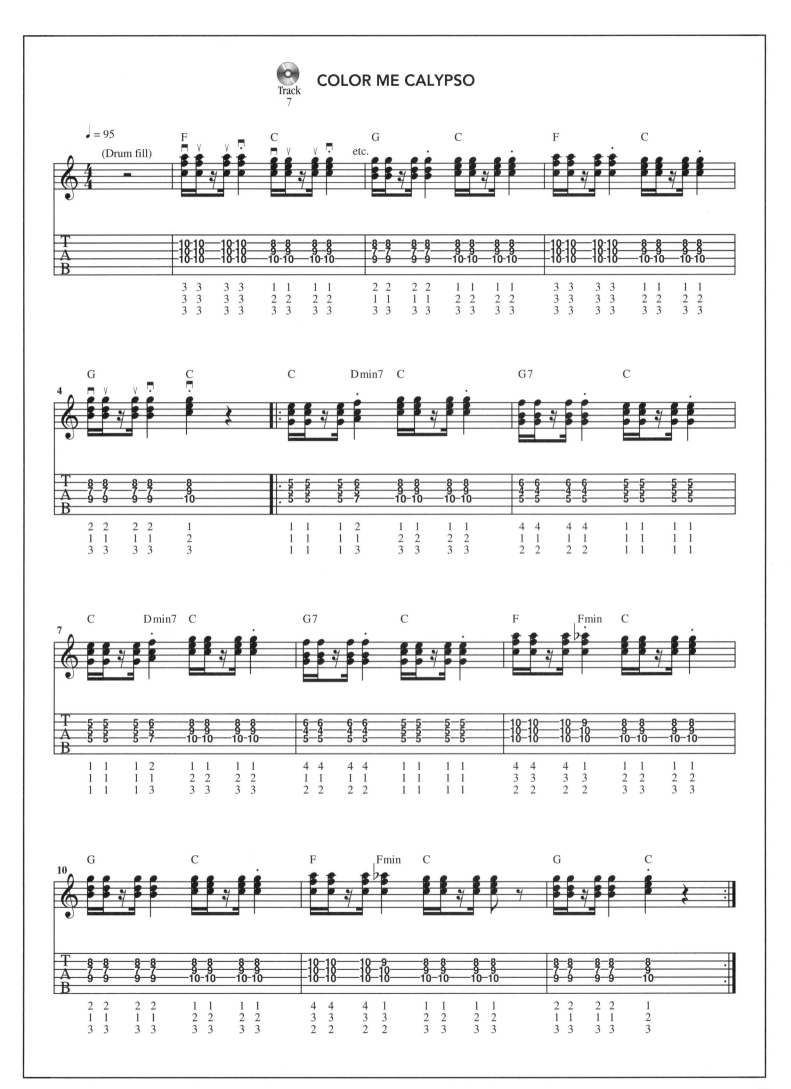

Chapter 2 SKA

JAMAICA

THE BEGINNINGS OF SKA

As mento's golden age waned in Jamaica, American R&B hits and early rock 'n' roll recordings exploded in Jamaican dancehalls known as *sound systems*. As the mento sound was fading out of popularity, American R&B and rock 'n' roll influences were becoming firmly assimilated into the Jamaican musical mainstream. By the early 1960s, Jamaican music had taken all of these influences and morphed them into something new, a fast and upbeat musical style called ska. Duke Reid and Clement "Coxone" Dodd, owners of two competing sound systems, saw a huge opportunity for growth. Reid and Dodd created the Treasure Isle and Studio One record labels, respectively, in order to produce exclusive recordings for their sound systems. Before long, the pressing plant Caribbean Records was established, and the Jamaican recording industry took off.

Ska was a huge success because it was such a danceable music; it fit in perfectly with the wildly popular Jamaican sound systems. It also reflected the newfound joy and optimism gained from Jamaica's independence in 1962. By 1964, ska had swept through Jamaica, and soon it would spread to England as well.

Let's take a look at the song that started it all: "Oh Carolina." When The Folkes Brothers went to RJR studios in 1960 to record, Jamaican producer (and former employee of Coxone Dodd) Prince Buster (Cecil Bustamente Campbell) brought in an unlikely rhythm section: Rastafari *Nyabinghi* (see page 40) drummers from the Wareika Hills of Jamaica, led by Jamaican drummer Count Ossie (Oswald Williams). The resulting number one hit song was called "Oh Carolina," and it is widely considered to be the tune that paved the way for the formation of ska. When playing the following piece, which is in the style of "Oh Carolina," take notice of the brisk tempo. Also, notice how the rhythm emphasizes the *offbeats;* this is known as *syncopation* and is a key component of the ska styles to follow. (The offbeat is the second half of a beat, or the "&;" see measures 5–9.)

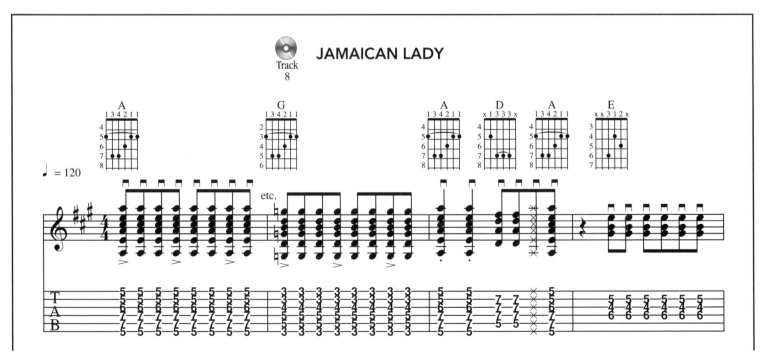

JAMAICAN LADY
Track 8

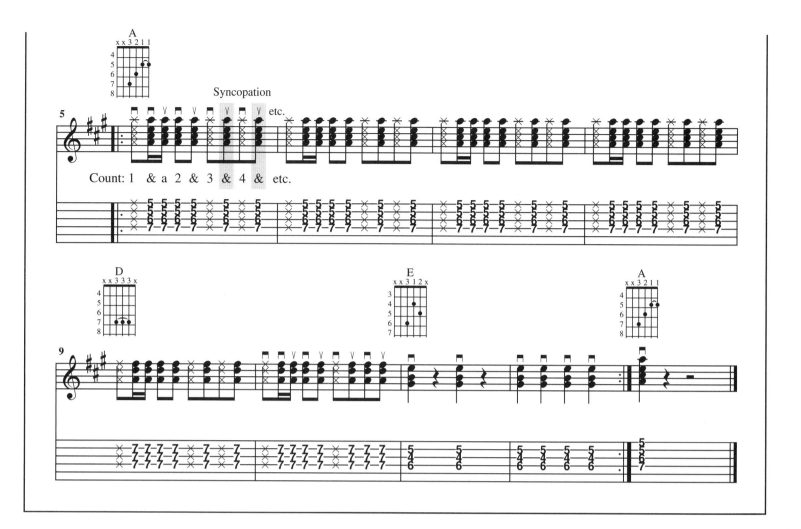

THE SKANK

The defining characteristic of ska guitar playing is a rhythm guitar technique called the *skank*. The skank was first used by the Jamaican guitarist Ernest Ranglin (see Chapter 6), who, while trying to imitate American R&B styles in the late 1950s, started strumming chords with sharp upstrokes on the offbeats of every measure. By the early 1960s, the skank had become a required technique for all ska guitarists (including Jerome "Jah Jerry" Haynes, a member of The Skatalites and a guitar student of Ernest Ranglin). Skanks are often played with three- or four-note chord voicings, and the upstrokes are usually preceded by muted downstrums played on the beats (1, 2, 3, 4, etc.). Ska music is sometimes played with a straight-eighth note feel and sometimes with a swing-eighth, or shuffle, feel. The following example illustrates a swing-eighth skank with a four-note voicing and muted downstrums.

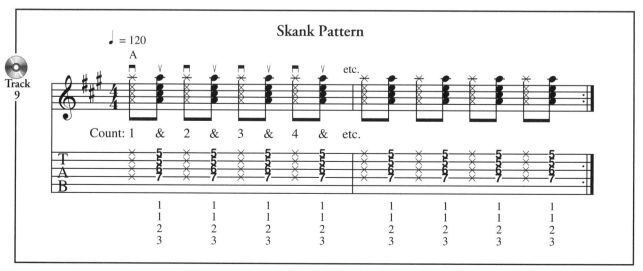

This following ska tune is in the style of "Forward March" by Derrick Morgan. "Forward March" holds an important place in Jamaican history not only because it was a hit on the charts, but also because it was the first emancipation song written in celebration of Jamaica's independence in 1962. In the early '60s, Derrick Morgan (who is still the only Jamaican artist to hold the top seven slots on the national pop-single charts simultaneously) was considered by many to be the "King of Ska." As the story goes, legendary Jamaican singer and producer Prince Buster recorded an instrumental break that was stolen from "Forward March," which set off an infamous, yet relatively shortlived, feud between the two. The arrangement below features the classic offbeat skank rhythm as well as some choice ska voicings.

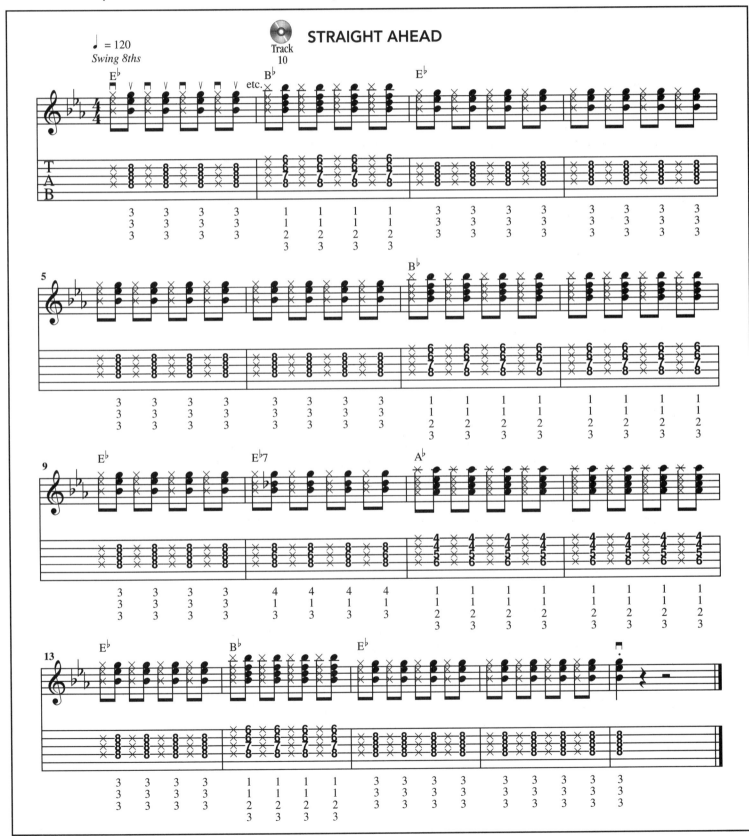

Below is a ska example arranged in the style of "I'll Never Grow Old" by The Maytals (who changed their name to Toots and The Maytals in 1972). This 1964 ska classic was produced by Coxone Dodd at Studio One. The recording featured the legendary backing band The Skatalites and a guest appearance by Ernest Ranglin on guitar. In the following example, you will be playing a straight-eighth skank, as well as some R&B-style dominant 9th chord voicings.

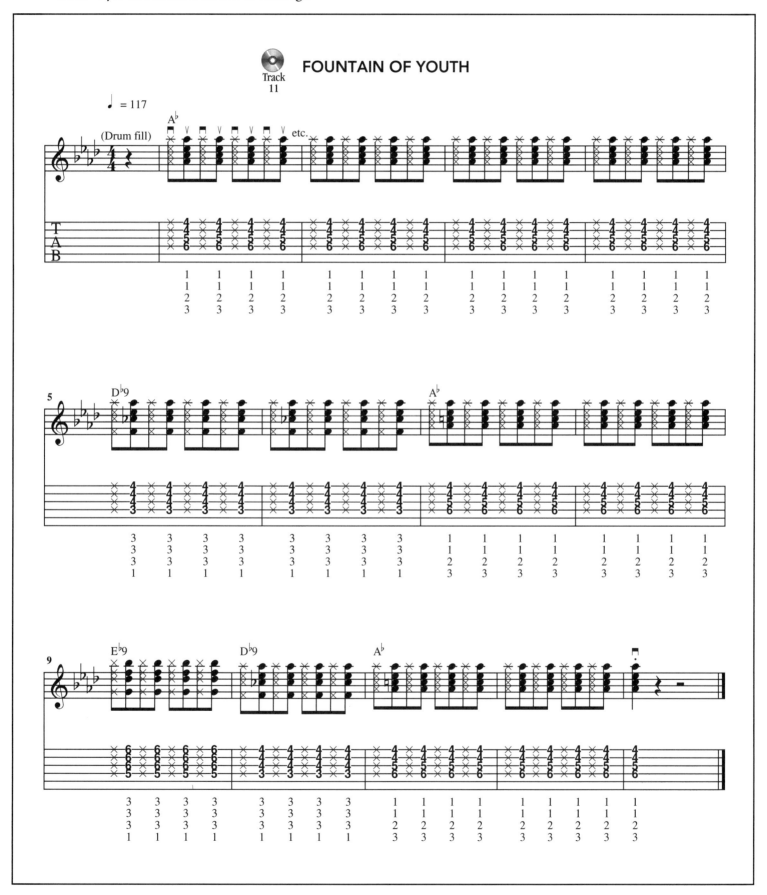

FOUNTAIN OF YOUTH

Track 11

SKA HORN LINES

One of the most distinct characteristics of ska music is the inclusion of a horn section. These horn sections play short, catchy melodies during intros and interludes, then often switch to offbeat chord *stabs,* along with the rhythm section, during the verses and choruses of the song. (A stab is a sharp, rhythmic "hit," or attack.) In the example below, a horn line in the style of the intro to "Simmer Down" by The Wailers has been arranged for guitar. The rhythm guitar in this example features an offbeat skank rhythm, a quickly changing chord progression, and three-note ska voicings.

The original tune "Simmer Down" was the first single released by The Wailers, recorded at Studio One by Coxone Dodd in 1963 (with the Skatalites backing them up in the rhythm section). It's a significant song not only because it was a number one hit in Jamaica in 1964, but also because it marked the start of the recording career of Bob Marley, one of the most influential musicians in the history of music.

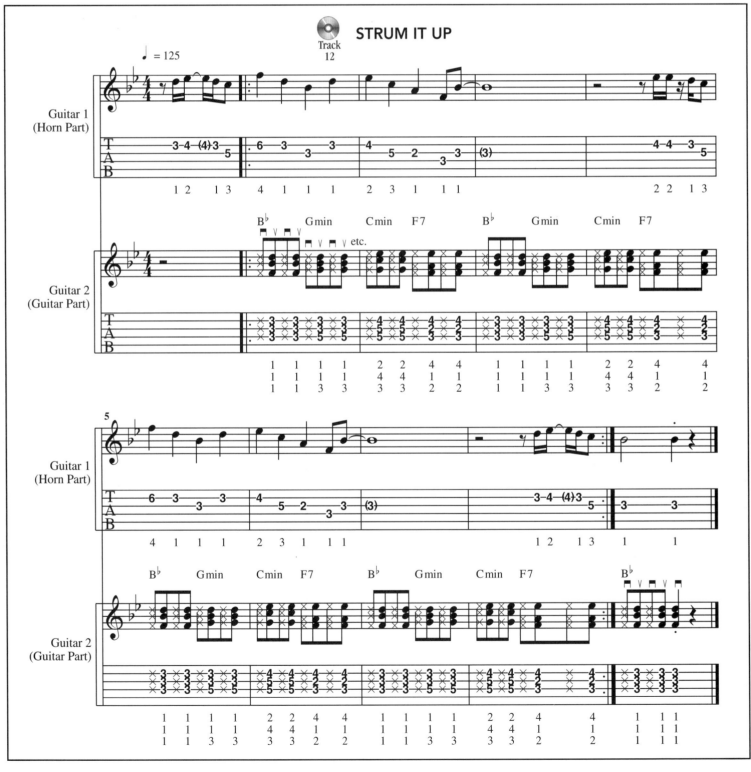

With a career spanning more than five decades, Laurel Aitken, known as the "Godfather of Ska," was Jamaica's first international recording star. Born in Cuba in 1927, Aitken moved to Jamaica (his father's homeland) when he was 11. He was winning talent competitions by age 15, and before long, he was a popular nightclub performer known for his wide range of singing and songwriting styles, including jump blues, R&B, calypso, and mento. In 1960, Laurel emigrated to England where he established himself as one of the key artists and producers developing Jamaican ska in the U.K. One of his biggest hits, "Rudi Got Married," was released in 1980 during the *2-Tone ska movement* in England (named after the English record label 2-Tone Records). By the late 1970s, a major revival of ska had emerged in England, which is why this 2-Tone period is also known as ska's *second wave.* The following example is written in the style of Laurel Aitken's second-wave ska classic "Rudi Got Married." It features three-note ska chords (voiced exclusively on the top three strings) and a harmonized horn melody arranged for guitar.

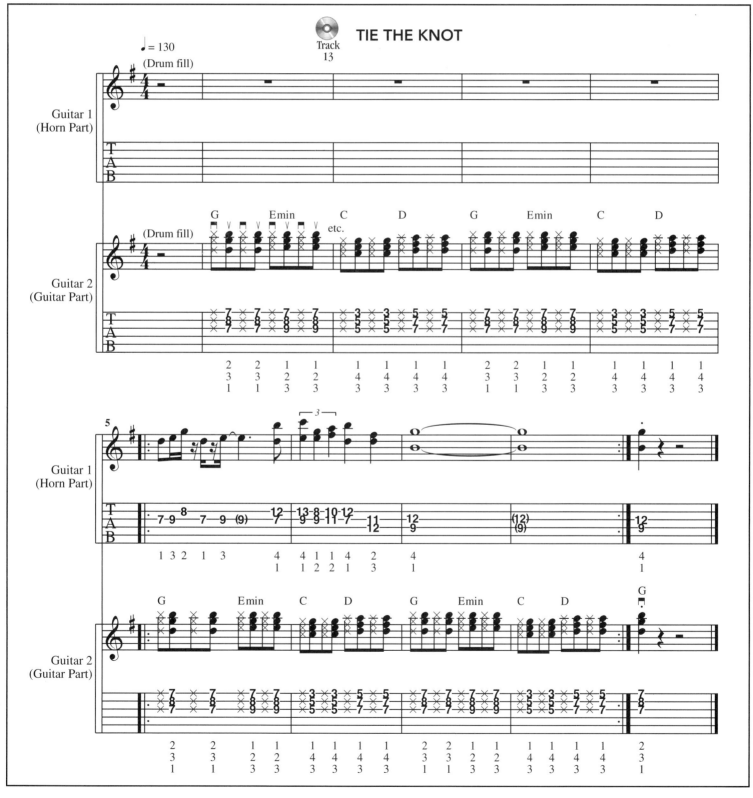

THE SKATALITES

Arguably, no other band defined and influenced the sound of ska more than The Skatalites. Formed in 1964, the original Skatalite lineup consisted of nine of Jamaica's top jazz musicians, including Tommy McCook on tenor sax and flute, Don Drummond on trombone, Rolando Alphonso on tenor sax, Lester Sterling on alto sax, Johnny Moore on trumpet, Lloyd Knibb on drums, Lloyd Brevett on bass, Jah Jerry Hains on guitar, and Jackie Mittoo on Piano and Organ. In addition, they were often joined by guitarists Ernest Ranglin and Nearlin "Lynn" Taitt in the studio.

Under such producers as Coxone Dodd, Duke Reid, Prince Buster, Leslie Kong, and Randy Chin, The Skatalites gained significant fame as the supergroup that backed most of the top Jamaican artists of the mid-1960s. Unfortunately, their first run was shortlived. Their trombonist, Don Drummond, was jailed and convicted for the murder of his girlfriend, which led to the breakup of the band by August of 1965 (Don died in prison four years later). Almost 20 years after their breakup, The Skatalites reformed in 1983 and have been going strong ever since.

This final ska example is representative of the current incarnation of The Skatalites, written in the style of "Flowers for Albert" from the 1994 Grammy-nominated album *Hi-Bop Ska*. The challenging rhythm guitar part combines both three- and four-note ska voicings with quickly moving chord changes and a key change halfway through the tune (in measure 14, the key changes from A Major to B♭ Major). Happy skanking!

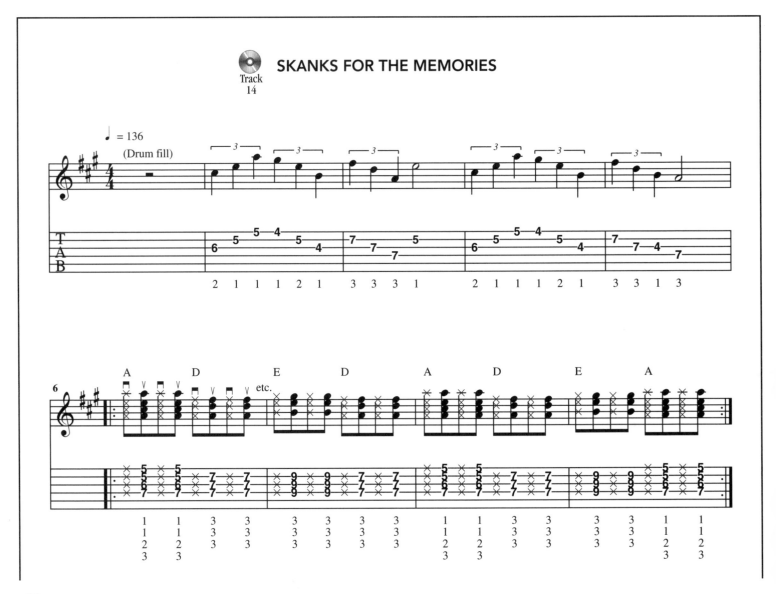

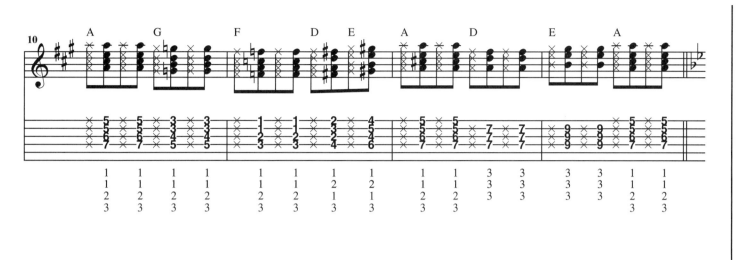

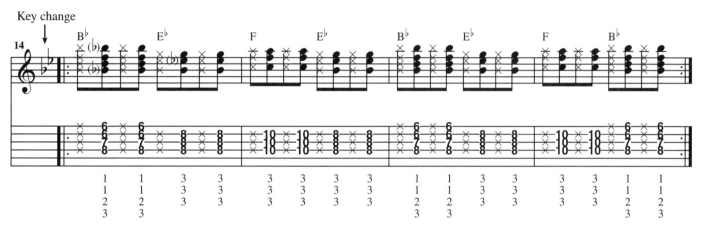

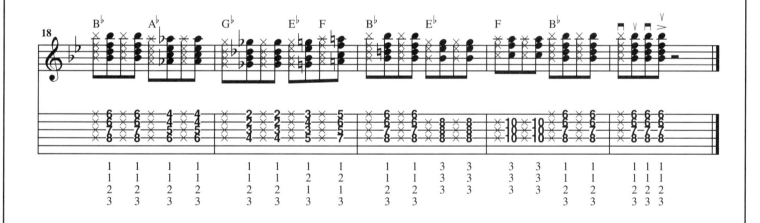

Chapter 3 ROCKSTEADY

JAMAICA

HISTORY OF ROCKSTEADY

Just as ska was born from the optimistic climate in Jamaica after gaining independence, a new type of music, rocksteady, reflected a growing dissatisfaction with the serious problems that remained. The youth who had flocked to the cities looking for opportunity often found themselves stuck in ghettos with no work or money; this led to a life of crime and gangs for many young Jamaicans. These *rude boys,* as they were called, had a wide impact on Jamaica's social structure, as well as the music scene. Through their cool style and often delinquent behavior, the rude boys' dissatisfaction with the quick tempo of ska became evident.

Before long, ska had run its course. By 1966, ska was replaced by the shortlived, yet enormously influential, musical style known as rocksteady. Rocksteady was a fairly drastic departure from ska, with a slower beat, no horn section, a more prominent bass line, and intricate vocal harmonies. Even though this style only lasted about two years, rocksteady left a profound mark on Jamaican music.

Figuring prominently in the history of rocksteady is guitar legend Lynn Taitt. Born in Trinidad, Lynn Taitt moved to Jamaica in 1962 and hit the ground running as a highly sought after session player. Four years later, Lynn Taitt was backing nearly every artist making records in Kingston. By the late 1960s, he had been involved in well over 1,500 recordings, distinguishing him as an unsung hero of Jamaican music. Lynn Taitt emigrated to Canada in August of 1968. Perhaps it is no coincidence that his departure coincided with the end of the rocksteady era.

SLOW IT DOWN

Alton Ellis, the "Godfather of Rocksteady," first started recording in an R&B style for Coxone Dodd at Studio One in 1959. By the mid-1960s, however, after a few years on the ska scene, Alton Ellis found his true calling as the undisputed leader of the new rocksteady movement. Alton started recording with Duke Reid's Treasure Isle label in 1965. One year later, he released a string of hits including "Girl I've Got a Date," which, according to many experts (including Alton himself), was the first rocksteady song ever recorded.

The example on the next page, in the style of "Girl I've Got a Date," retains a hint of the momentum of ska due to the offbeat strums. However, the slower tempo creates a much more relaxed feel. Also, notice the melodic emphasis on the bass line, which is doubled by the guitar (Guitar 2). This doubling technique is used often and is one of rocksteady's distinguishing characteristics.

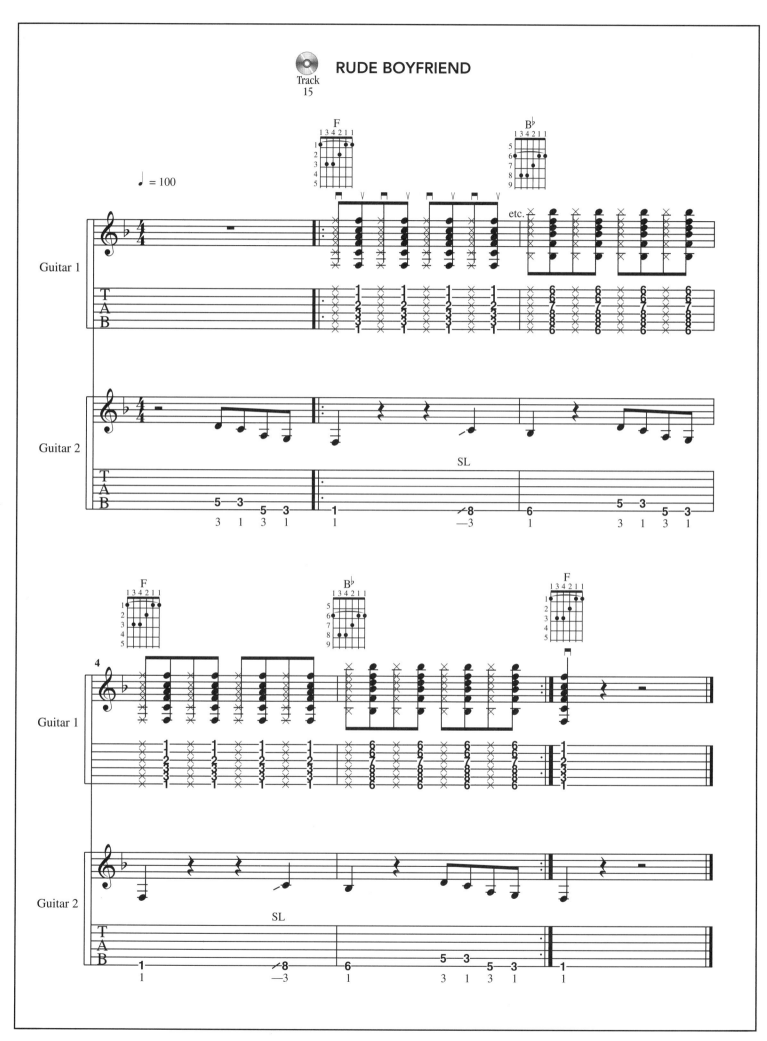

RUDE BOYFRIEND

Below is an example in the style of "Get Ready Rock Steady" by Alton Ellis. By all accounts, this 1967 masterpiece coined the term "rocksteady." Produced by Duke Reid's Treasure Isle label, Alton was backed by Tommy McCook & The Supersonics (with Lynn Taitt on guitar). It's a great example because the original track perfectly captured the essence of Lynn Taitt's syncopated percussive guitar intros. In order to emulate Lynn Taitt's electric guitar sound, set your amp for a clean tone with a bit of reverb. Then, place a heavy palm mute on each note in Guitar 1 to get a staccato sound (this is accomplished by placing the heel of your right hand on the strings where they meet the bridge). Also, due to the relatively leisurely tempo of this rocksteady tune, the rhythm guitar part (Guitar 2) is played with sharp downstrums rather than ska-style upstrokes.

KEEP IT MUTED

This example is written in the style of the first rocksteady hit, "Take It Easy" by Hopeton Lewis, which was released in late 1966. This early rocksteady tune helped signal a clean break from ska not only by relaxing the tempo, but also by the lyrics, which tell the listener to literally "Take It Easy." The rhythm section for the original track was, no surprise, Lynn Taitt and his group The Jets (although it is said that Ernest Ranglin was on this session as well). As is often the case with Lynn Taitt-style riffs, the guitar begins with a palm-muted melodic intro that is doubled on the bass. Then, for the main body of the tune, offbeat chord strums are played, except for the few instances where chord changes are anticipated by slides (see measures 4 and 5, for example).

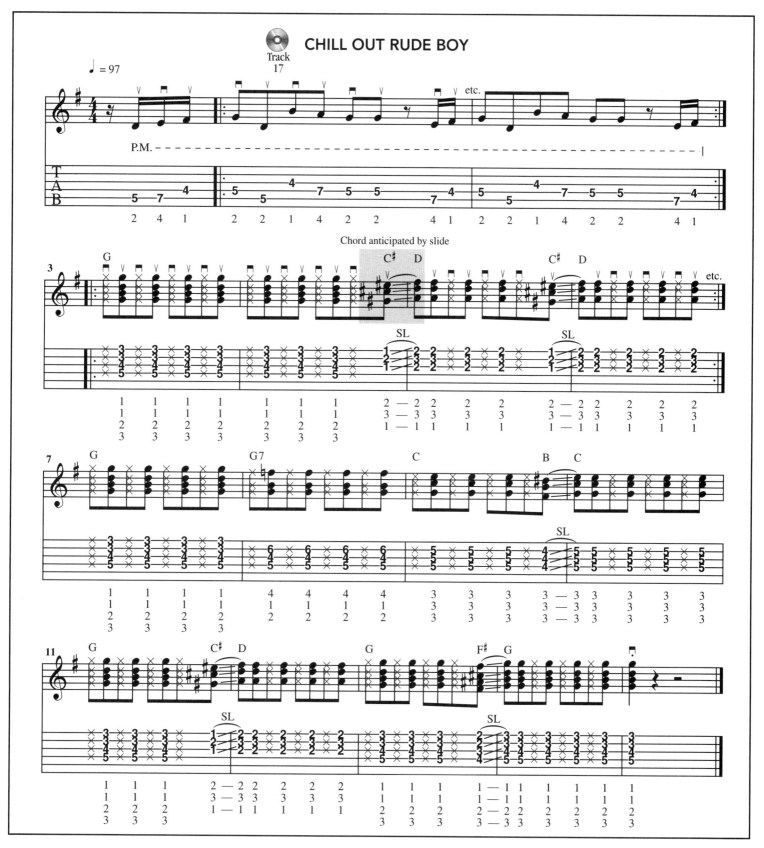

CHILL OUT RUDE BOY

STEADY SIXTEENTHS

Jamaican singer, songwriter, and stage showman Roy Shirley (born Ainsworth Roy Rushton in 1944) was known both as King Roy Shirley and The High Priest. His 1967 hit song "Hold Them" is considered one of the formative tunes that solidified rocksteady as a new movement. In the style of "Hold Them," the example below features a more active Lynn Taitt-style of guitar playing. One benefit of rocksteady's slower tempo is that there is more space available for the development of guitar and bass melodies. In particular, notice how the addition of sixteenth-note embellishments sound surprisingly laid back when combined with the relaxed rocksteady beat.

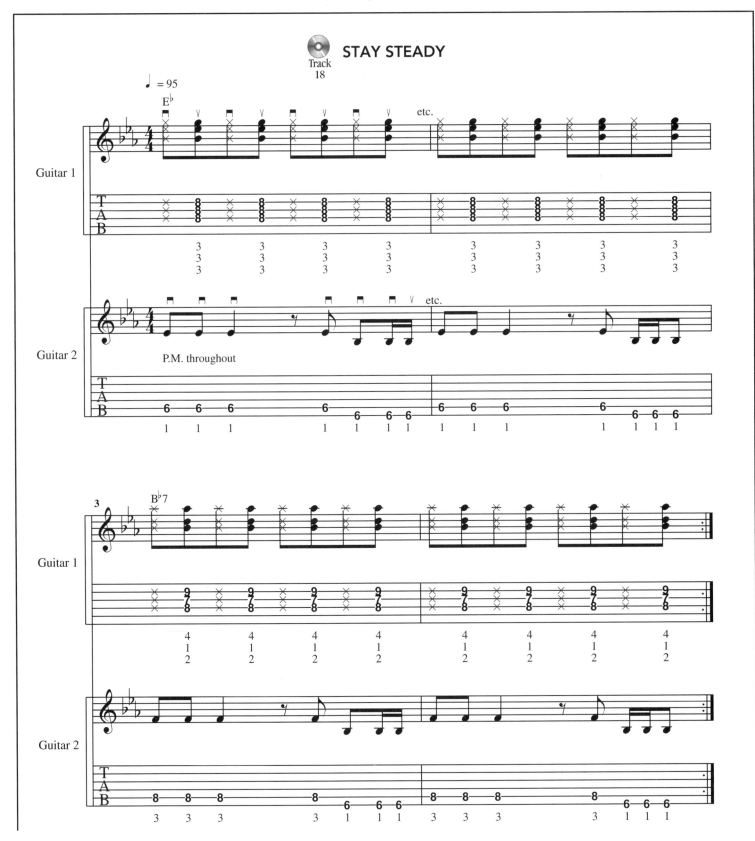

By the late 1960s, the musical winds of change were starting to blow in Jamaica. Rocksteady was quickly morphing into reggae. A prime example of a rocksteady song that started to show clear reggae traits is "ABC Rocksteady," recorded by the Jamaican vocal trio The Gaylads. Produced by Sonia Pottinger, this song was one of the first with an authentic reggae beat (it featured a *one-drop* rhythm, covered on page 31). The following example is written in the style of the 1968 rocksteady classic "ABC Rocksteady," highlighting Lynn Taitt's percussive palm-muted sixteenth-note style. The sixteenth notes in Guitar 2 are to be played with a swing feel (*Swing 16ths*). Swing sixteenths are played like sixteenth-note triplets with the first two sixteenths tied (♫ = ♫♫).

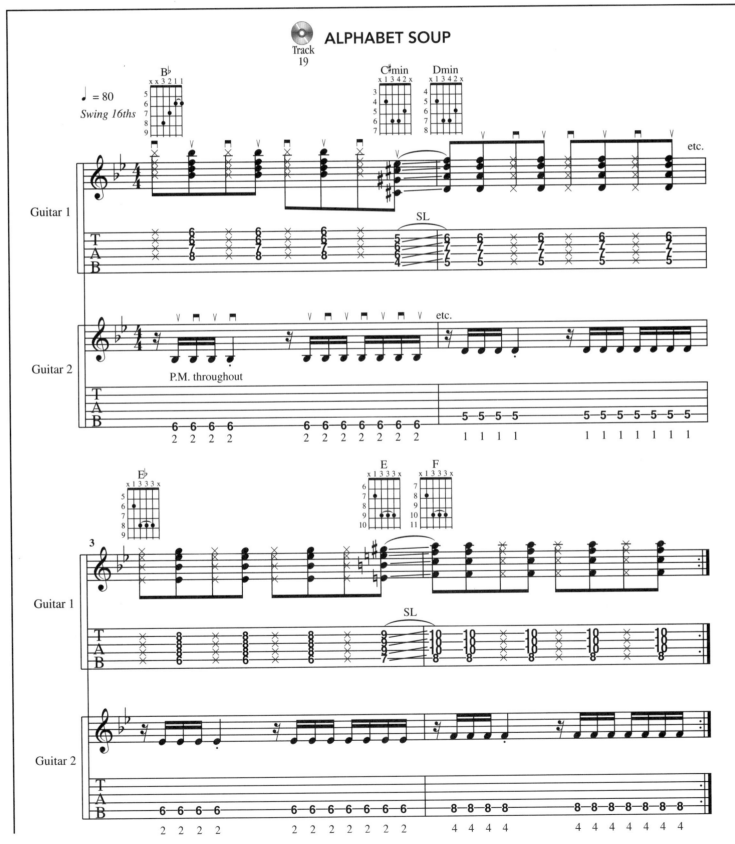

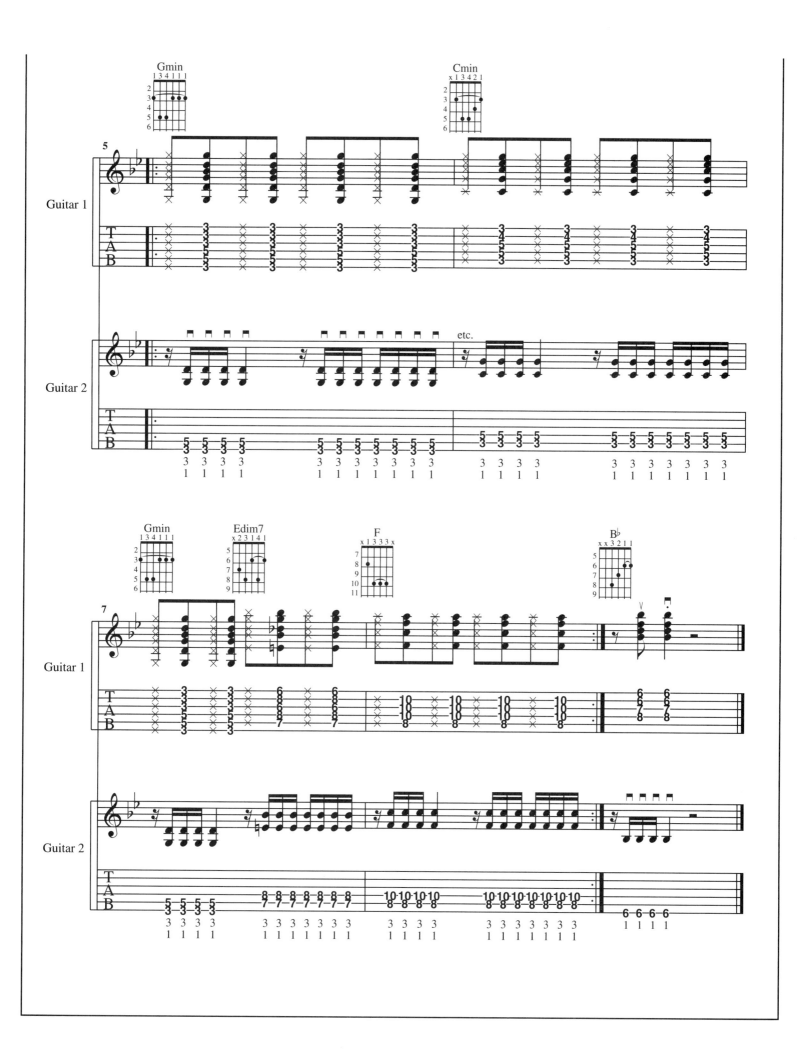

Chapter 4 REGGAE

JAMAICA

EARLY REGGAE

At the end of the 1960s, with the influence of traditional African music, Caribbean music, American R&B, and, most importantly, ska and rocksteady, Jamaican music evolved yet again. The result was reggae, a form that defined an entire generation of Jamaican music. Starting in 1968, early reggae began working its way into Jamaican popular music alongside *dub* and *toasting*. Although reggae, dub, and toasting are all distinct Jamaican art forms, they are deeply connected. Essentially, dub is a style that involves the remixing of existing tunes, over which the deejay toasts. Toasting is a precursor to rapping, in which the deejay talks and rhymes in a half-sung, rhythmic way in an effort to motivate the audience to dance.

Starting in the 1960s, a key component of both the music and the music business in Jamaica was the concept of the *riddim*. On a practical level, the riddim is the groove created by the specific drum and bass riff of a given tune. However, the term "riddim" also refers to the background, or rhythm section, portion of the song used by deejays for toasting—or as the basis for an entirely new song (otherwise known as a *version*). Due to the nonexistent copyright laws in Jamaica at the time (Jamaican copyright laws weren't enacted until 1993), and the speed with which these versions could be created, it's easy to see why Jamaican music spread so quickly: one riddim might be used on hundreds of tunes! This chapter looks at the music of some of the most prominent reggae artists from the early '70s to the mid-'80s, including examples in the style of a few highly "versioned" riddims, like the one that follows.

The example below is written in the style of the 1971 hit single "Cherry Oh Baby" by singer-songwriter Eric Donaldson. This tune, which is considered a milestone in the development of the reggae genre, highlights some of the stylistic differences between reggae and its musical predecessors. In particular, notice the stark simplicity of the rhythm section. The unison starting and stopping of the guitar, bass, and drums creates a focused emphasis on the riddim. With this pared-down arrangement (no horns, background singers, or lead guitars), the original "Cherry Oh Baby" tune is one of the most heavily used riddims ever, having laid the foundation for over 100 tunes and remixes!

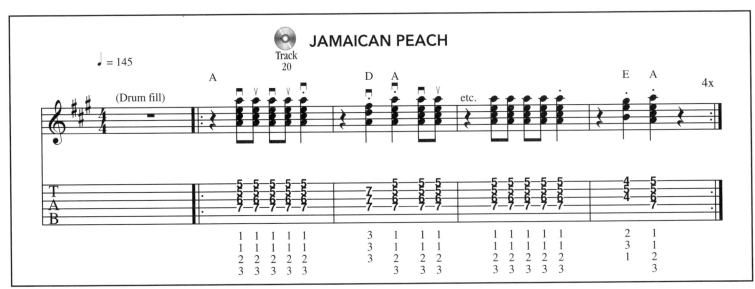

JAMAICAN PEACH — Track 20

Throughout 1972 and 1973, Jamaican singer Jimmy Cliff was thrown into the spotlight as the star of the film *The Harder They Come*. Based on the story of a real-life Jamaican criminal from the late 1940s, the movie and the hit soundtrack brought reggae to a whole new level of international popularity.

The following example, based on Jimmy Cliff's title song on the soundtrack from *The Harder They Come,* illustrates a close interaction between the organ and the rhythm guitar that is common in reggae music. Guitar 1 is the organ part arranged for guitar, and Guitar 2 maintains a palm-muted sixteenth-note pulse throughout. Also present in this example is one of the most defining characteristics of reggae music, the *one-drop* rhythm. A one-drop rhythm is created when the drummer, playing in $\frac{4}{4}$ time, simultaneously plays a snare drum stroke and a bass drum kick on the third beat of every measure. As you listen to Track 21 on your CD, shift your attention to the drums for an example of the one-drop rhythm in action.

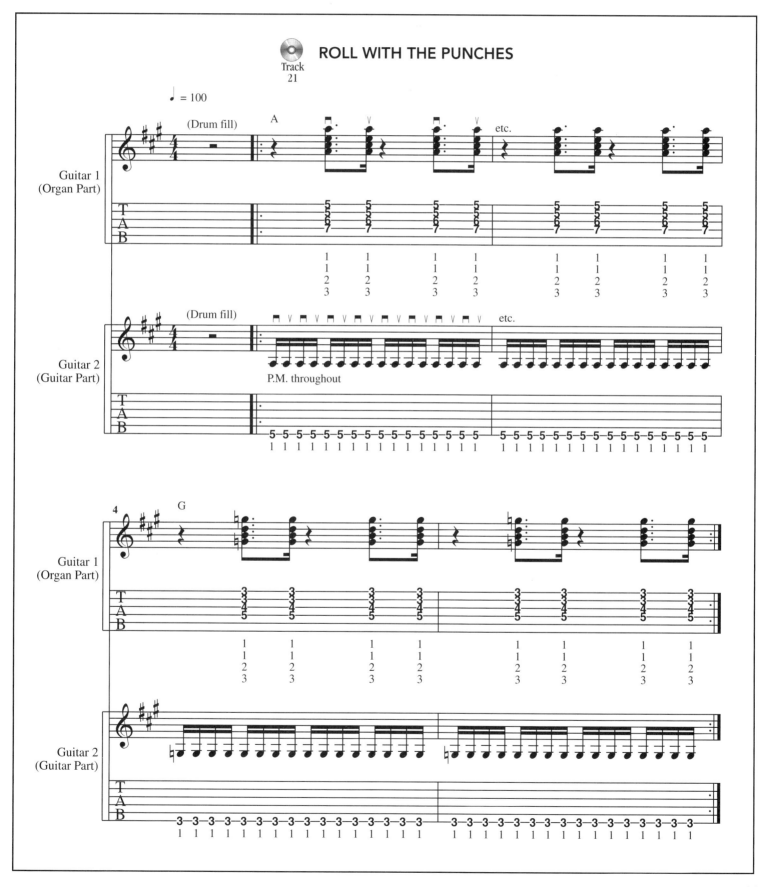

Dennis Brown (known as the "Crown Prince of Reggae") was one of Jamaica's most beloved and prolific artists, recording over 75 albums during his career. In 1973, Dennis Brown's early reggae classic "Westbound Train" was number one on the Jamaican charts. Interestingly, the intro and interlude of the original "Westbound Train" featured a verbatim guitar riff from Al Green's classic tune "Love and Happiness." Produced by Winston "Niney" Holness, this tune featured the masterful guitar work of Earl "Chinna" Smith and Tony Chin from Soul Syndicate (Niney's house band). The example below is in the style of "Westbound Train." It begins with staccato offbeat strums played by the rhythm guitar, to which is added a sixteenth-note lead guitar riff.

32

THE RASTAFARI MOVEMENT AND ROOTS REGGAE

The Rastafari movement began with the philosophies of Jamaican black nationalist Marcus Garvey, who, in the 1920s, promoted the Universal Negro Improvement Association (UNIA). In 1927, Marcus Garvey, who had recently been deported from the United States back to Jamaica, spread the word that African redemption would come through the crowning of a new king of Ethiopia. In 1930, Ras Tafari Makonnen was crowned Haile Selassie, the new Emperor of Ethiopia, which was seen by many as fulfillment of Marcus Garvey's prophecy. This led to the belief that Haile Selassie was Jah (Jehovah, or God) reincarnate. Rastas believe that Jah lives within the human body in the form of the holy spirit; this is why they often refer to themselves as "I and I." However, the Rastafari movement is not considered an organized religion, but rather, a way of life.

In the 1950s, the Rastafari lived on the fringes of society. They were looked down upon in mainstream Jamaica due to their dreadlocks and beards (Rastas didn't comb or cut their hair because of their belief that the body must remain whole) and their ritualistic use of cannabis, or marijuana. As reggae became increasingly influenced by Rastafari culture and concerns, the term *roots reggae* was coined. The last half of the 1970s is generally considered the golden era of roots reggae. During this time, bands and artists like Bob Marley, Burning Spear, Horace Andy, Black Uhuru, and The Abyssinians popularized roots reggae and brought the Rasta belief system to the international stage. At its heart, roots reggae is a spiritual music primarily concerned with issues such as peace, poverty, government oppression, Afrocentric repatriation, and the worship of Jah through the Rastafari tradition. Largely through the influence of Bob Marley, the Rastafari movement has spread throughout much of the world. Today, there are estimated to be over one million Rasta living worldwide, however, only about five to ten percent of Jamaicans identify themselves as Rastafari.

THE "BUBBLE"

It is very common for roots reggae keyboard players to create what is called a "bubbling" effect by playing their chords with an alternating left-hand, right-hand, left-hand pattern. In the example on the next page, Guitar 2 is an arrangement of this "bubbling" keyboard style. Instead of playing an alternating left-hand, right-hand, left-hand pattern like a keyboard, a similar effect is created on the guitar with a bass-chord-bass pattern. Although this technique can be accomplished with a pick (as it is notated here), it can also be played fingerstyle, assigning the thumb to the bass notes, and the index, middle, and ring fingers to the top notes of the chords.

The example on the next page is in the style of the song "Slavery Days" from the groundbreaking 1975 album *Marcus Garvey* released by reggae legend Burning Spear. The guitar players on this album were Earl "Chinna" Smith and Tony Chin, who were supported by a top-shelf rhythm section that included Robbie Shakespeare on bass and Leroy "Horsemouth" Wallace on drums. Born Winston Rodney in 1948 in St. Ann, Jamaica, Burning Spear is a two-time Grammy Award winner (he has been nominated for a total of 12 Grammys) and is a devout Rastafari.

NEVER FORGET

Track 23

Released as a single in 1971, The Abyssinians' reggae classic "Satta Massagana" is one of the first African-oriented reggae tunes and a frequently versioned riddim. It's a classic roots reggae song not just because of the spiritual overtones of the lyrics (which are partly sung in the Ethiopian Amharic language), but also because it provides another opportunity to examine the tight, rhythmic interaction between the guitar and keyboards. The following example is written in the style of "Satta Massagana." Guitar 1 plays downstrums on beats 2 and 4, while Guitar 2 is an arrangement of the offbeat keyboard line. Notice how the two parts interlock, with the strums of Guitar 1 alternating with the offbeat strums of Guitar 2. This interaction creates a syncopated, rhythmic bubbling effect similar to the example on the previous page.

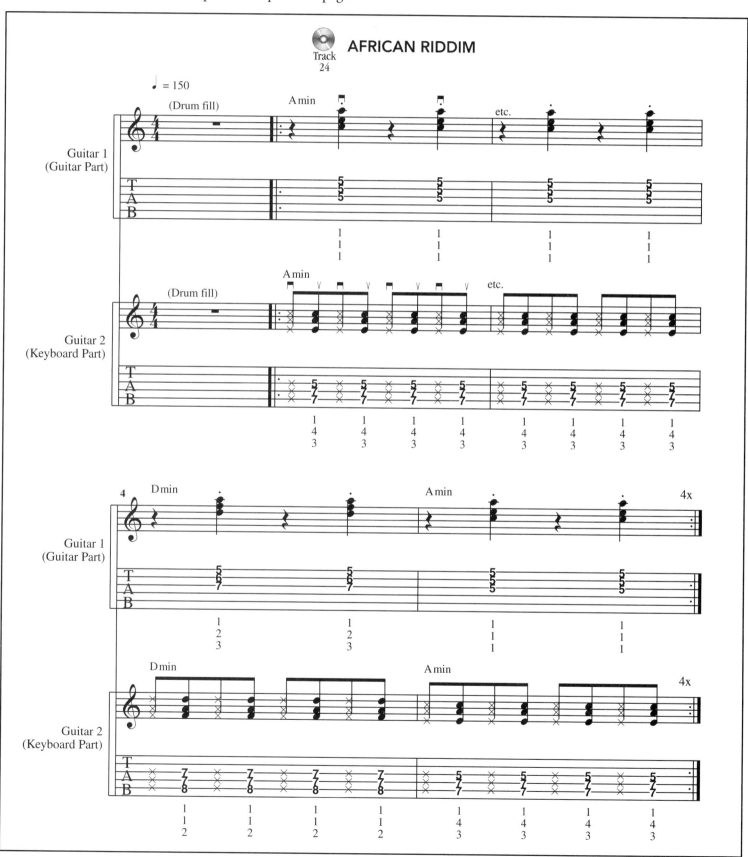

REGGAE RHYTHM EMBELLISHMENT

One of the most distinctive vocalists to emerge from the Jamaican music scene is Horace Andy. Born Horace Hinds in Kingston, Jamaica in 1951, "Sleepy" Horace Andy is known for his high tenor voice and pronounced vibrato. The following example is in the style of "Child of the Ghetto," a tune recorded in the early 1970s at Studio One, but not released until the 1998 Horace Andy compilation *Mr. Bassie*. This example illustrates an effective technique for embellishing a basic roots reggae rhythm guitar part. The trick is for the rhythm guitar to add an eighth-note upstroke on the "&" of beats 2 and 4, frequently holding this chord over for the next beat. Then, every once in a while, this upstrum is held over the barline (see measures 4 and 5). When used sparingly, this can be an effective device, especially when contrasted with staccato sixteenth notes played by a second guitar.

BACK ALLEY DREADLOCK

DUB-STYLE EFFECTS

Black Uhuru ("uhuru" is the Swahili word for freedom) is one of the most internationally successful Jamaican roots reggae bands. In 1985, they were the first artists to win a Grammy in the newly introduced reggae category for their hit song "What Is Life?" This song, like many Black Uhuru tunes, has a fairly progressive sound, with American pop-rock and Jamaican dub influences.

The example on the next page is in the style of Black Uhuru's song "What Is Life?" It features the use of *echo,* a remix trick common in Jamaican dub recordings involving a delay effect. On the accompanying CD, Guitar 1 is running through a *delay pedal* with the repeat set roughly to a quarter-note triplet pattern. (A delay pedal records the signal from the guitar and plays it back at various speeds and volumes.) Guitar 2 is going through a *chorus pedal,* giving it a shimmering pop-rock tone. (A chorus pedal takes the guitar signal and combines it with delayed copies of itself that have been altered in pitch). On the original recording, prolific reggae gurus Sly Dunbar (drums) and Robbie Shakespeare (bass) laid down their rhythm section magic, giving this recording what is known as a *rocker's beat.* Rocker's reggae drum beats usually contain a heavy kick-drum accent on beat 1, in addition to the usual one-drop accent on beat 3.

THE QUESTION

Chapter 5 BOB MARLEY

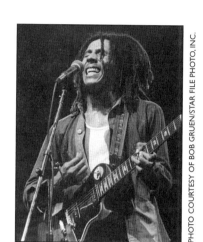

JAMAICA

More than anyone, Robert "Bob" Nesta Marley, born in Saint Ann, Jamaica in 1945, was the cultural icon that made Jamaican music an international sensation. By the time of his death in 1981, Bob Marley had survived an assassination attempt, toured the world three times, fathered 12 children (two were adopted), composed hundreds of songs (many of which are considered archetypal masterpieces), received Jamaica's Order of Merit Award, received the United Nations Medal of Peace on behalf of five-hundred million Africans, brought international attention to the Rastafarian faith, and inspired millions of people with a deeply spiritual message of peace through music.

A testament to his world-wide popularity, the compilation album *Legend,* released three years after his death, went platinum 10 times over in the U.S. alone, becoming the best-selling reggae album in history. All in all, Bob Marley's accomplishments are truly amazing considering he only lived to be 36. In fact, his superstar status, gifted vocal ability, and brilliant songwriting make it easy to overlook the fact that he was also an excellent guitar player. But ultimately, through all of the fame and fortune, he remained a humble artist, spreading a positive message and a peaceful vision of humanity. This chapter examines a few of the Bob Marley masterpieces that helped reggae become a world-wide phenomenon.

Bob Marley (1945–1981).

IN THE STYLE OF "STIR IT UP"

This example is written in the style of "Stir It Up," composed by Bob Marley in 1967. The song was popularized by pop singer-songwriter Johnny Nash in 1972. Released a year later on The Wailers' *Catch a Fire* album, "Stir It Up" proved to be one of Bob Marley's biggest international hits. The example below features a classic reggae one-drop beat, with Guitar 1 laying down eighth-note strums on beats 2 and 4, and Guitar 2 doubling the bass line.

IN THE STYLE OF "RASTA MAN CHANT"

The next example is written in the style of "Rasta Man Chant" from the 1973 *Burnin'* album by The Wailers. The original recording of "Rasta Man Chant" was based on Nyabinghi drum ceremonies. Nyabinghi ceremonies are Rastafarian gatherings in which the celebrants praise Jah through chant, dance, and sacred drumming. The Nyabinghi rhythm emphasizes two eighth-note strums on beats 1 and 3, creating a heartbeat rhythm. Notice the similarity with the previous example, where the same strums are placed on beats 2 and 4. As in the previous example, Guitar 2 doubles the bass.

IN THE STYLE OF "I SHOT THE SHERIFF"

The Wailers' fourth major-label album, *Burnin'*, is significant because it was the last album The Wailers released before co-founders Peter Tosh and Bunny Wailer left the group to pursue solo careers (at which point the band became known as Bob Marley and The Wailers). Plus, it featured "I Shot the Sheriff," a tune that became an international hit due largely to Eric Clapton's cover version. Clapton's "I Shot the Sheriff" was a number one hit on the American charts, which helped propel Bob Marley even further into international fame. The example on the next page is written in the style of "I Shot the Sheriff," and it features a longer song form and simple three-note chord voicings.

IN THE STYLE OF "EXODUS"

In late 1976, Bob Marley agreed to perform in Smile Jamaica, an outdoor concert organized by Michael Manley, the Prime Minister of Jamaica. Unfortunately, agreeing to appear in this concert proved dangerous, because two days before the show, Bob Marley, his wife, and manager were shot at Marley's home in a politically motivated assassination attempt. Thankfully, everyone survived, but after this incident, Bob and his family immediately relocated to London, where he recorded what many people consider his most groundbreaking album, *Exodus.* Released in 1977, at the height of the British punk movement, *Exodus* was a huge international success. In addition to being their first gold album, Exodus received widespread critical acclaim, so much so that in 1998, Time magazine voted it the best music album of the 20th century.

The following example is in the style of the title track of the *Exodus* album. It's a Bob Marley classic that features what is known as a *steppers,* or "four to the floor," rhythm. The defining characteristic of the steppers beat is that the drummer plays the kick drum on all four quarter notes of the measure, which gives a momentum and urgency to the beat. The guitar is playing a syncopated rhythm figure that accents every third eighth-note strum. Immediately after the accented strum, lift up your fretting finger slightly (still touching the string) to create a fret-hand mute. To get a tone similar to the original recording, pick your muted chords with quick and choppy strums. The effect is a washboard-like raking sound.

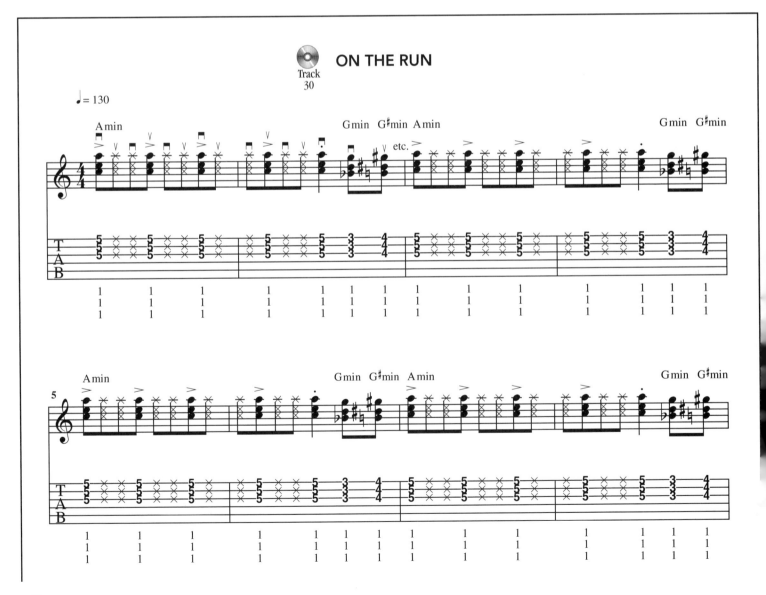

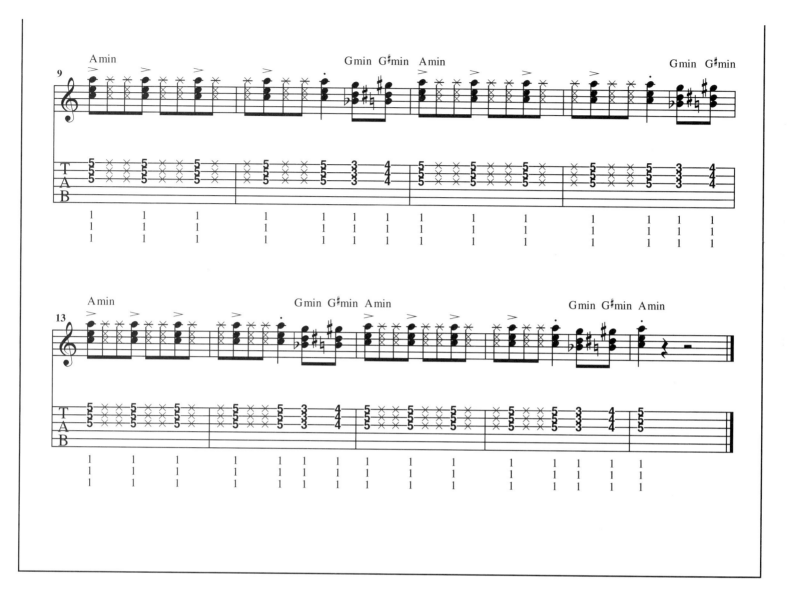

IN THE STYLE OF "REDEMPTION SONG"

Bob Marley was diagnosed with cancer in July of 1977, only a month after *Exodus* was released. Amazingly, even with the knowledge of his illness and deteriorating health, Bob Marley released three more studio albums: *Kaya* in 1978, *Survival* in 1979, and *Uprising* in 1980. *Uprising* was a particularly important work, in part because it was the last studio album Bob Marley ever recorded, and it also featured the tune that some believe was his greatest composition, the last track on the album, "Redemption Song."

The example on the next page, written in the style of "Redemption Song," features a single-note melodic introduction, and a folk-style strumming pattern on the acoustic guitar. The original "Redemption Song" is an excellent example of melodic and harmonic simplicity, serving as a backdrop for brilliant lyrical content that is both deeply personal and, at the same time, universally inclusive. "Redemption Song" is the last song he ever performed before his passing in 1981. It is fitting that the career of master musician, songwriter, and cultural icon Bob Marley would conclude gracefully with a simple folk song.

RASTA FAREWELL

Chapter 6   ERNEST RANGLIN

JAMAICA

Since this book focuses on the music of Jamaica from a guitar player's perspective, it's fitting to conclude by acknowledging one of Jamaica's truly legendary guitar players, Ernest Ranglin. Born in Manchester, Jamaica in 1932, this self-taught guitarist was well known in Jamaica as a rising star by the age of 16. In 1948, Ernest Ranglin joined his first group, the Val Bennett Orchestra, which played at local Jamaican hotels. His reputation grew quickly, and two years later, he was a member of one of Jamaica's best known big bands, the Eric Deans Orchestra, touring the Caribbean extensively and playing in the best hotels.

By the late 1950s and early '60s, Ernest was leading the way in developing the ska sound. His recordings for Island Records and Studio One are considered classics that influenced generations of musicians. In the '60s, he was in constant demand as a versatile guitarist and arranger. By the 1970s, Ernest had recorded with Millie Small (on her hit "My Boy Lollypop"), The Melodians, The Wailers, The Skatalites, Toots and The Maytals, and Jimmy Cliff just to name a few. Plus, Bob Marley had asked Ernest to be his live-in guitar teacher!

However, the true magic of Ernest Ranglin is that he has continued recording up to this day, pushing the boundaries of style by melding jazz, ska, reggae, and world music into a fusion all his own. To demonstrate this eclectic mix, our final example ("The Journey Begins" on the next page) features a layering of three independent guitar parts. This example is written in the style of a tune called "D'accord Dakar," the first track on the 1998 album *In Search of the Lost Riddim*, recorded in Senegal with the famous African singer Baaba Maal and his band.

The form of "The Journey Begins" is repeated five times. The first time through, only Guitar 3 is playing; the second time through, Guitars 2 and 3 are playing; and the third, fourth, and fifth times through, all three guitars are playing. On your CD, Track 32 features all three guitars. Track 33 consists of only Guitars 2 and 3, so you can take the part of Guitar 1. Track 34 consists of only Guitars 1 and 3, so you can take the part of Guitar 2. Track 35 consists of only Guitars 1 and 2, so you can take the part of Guitar 3. Have fun with this Ernest Ranglin-style arrangement!

PHOTO BY ADRIAN BOOT/COURTESY OF URBANIMAGE.TV

Ernest Ranglin (b. 1932) was a major force in the creation of ska in the late 1950s. Perhaps the most innovative guitarist in Jamaica's history, Ranglin made his first guitar out of a sardine can and wires. Known for fusing Jamaican styles such as ska and reggae with jazz and world styles, Ranglin has performed and recorded with many artists including The Wailers, Jimmy Cliff, Prince Buster, The Skatalites, and jazz saxophonist Sonny Stitt.

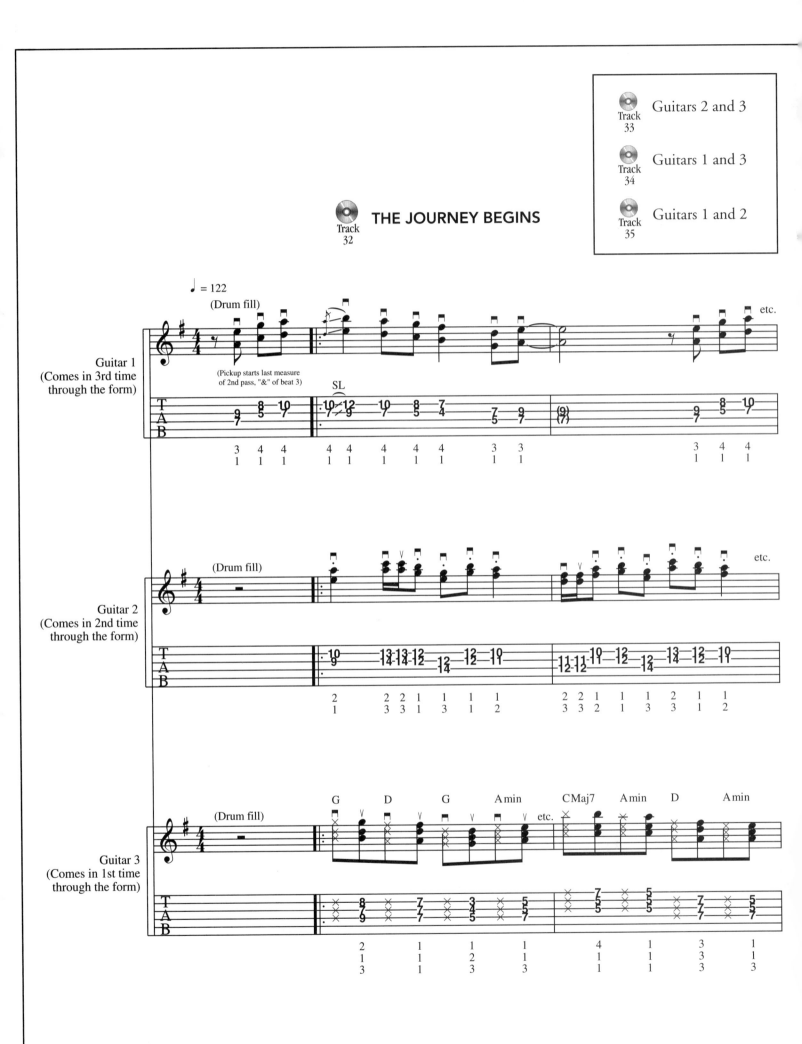

THE JOURNEY BEGINS

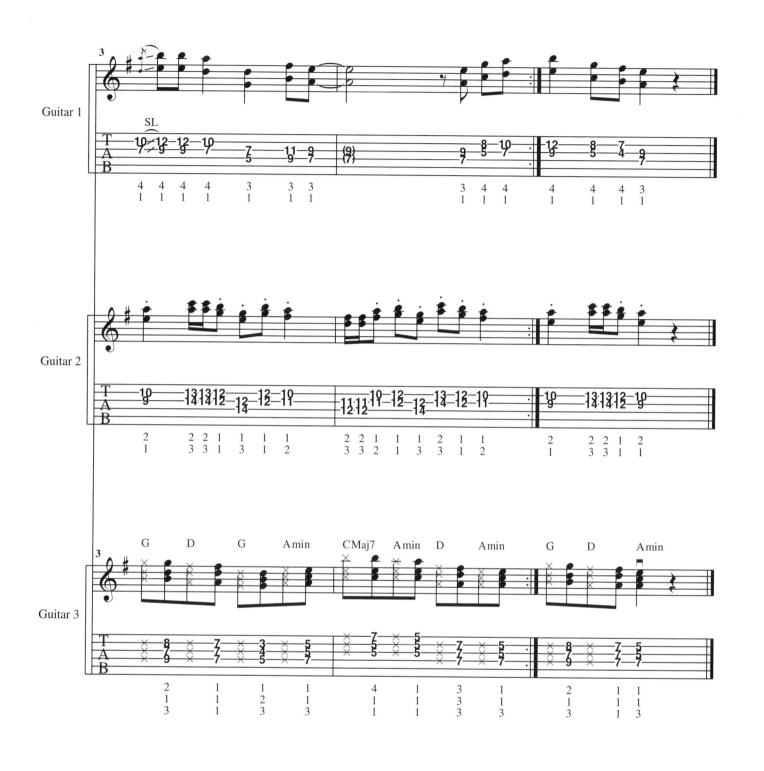

CONCLUSION

I hope you have enjoyed this book, and it has given you a deeper appreciation for the rich tradition of Jamaican music. I encourage you to continue your own explorations by listening to and learning more about the artists covered here, also by applying the techniques and concepts that you've learned to your own playing. Jamaican music is here for all of us to enjoy. Peace.